Ugh! Yuck! and Whoa!

Don't Bite Me!

WORLD
BOOK

World Book, Inc.
180 North LaSalle Street
Suite 900
Chicago, Illinois 60601
USA

For information about other World Book publications, visit our website at **www.worldbook.com** or call **1-800-WORLDBK (967-5325)**.

Library of Congress Cataloging-in-Publication data has been applied for.
Title: Ugh! Yuck! and Whoa! Don't Bite Me!
ISBN: 978-0-7166-3710-3

Ugh! Yuck! and Whoa!
ISBN: 978-0-7166-3708-0 (set, hc)

Also available as:
ISBN: 978-0-7166-3718-9 (e-book)

1st printing July 2018

Introduction

Nature is filled with some amazing creatures. From ocean bottoms to mountain tops, from hot deserts to freezing tundra, the *Ugh! Yuck! and Whoa!* books highlight the most extreme animals: the grossest, the deadliest, the strangest, and the ugliest! This book is all about animals with crazy teeth and dangerous bites. Strange **adaptations** in mouths of animals help them to survive. An **adaptation** is something an animal or other living thing has or does that helps it survive and reproduce (make more living things like itself) in its environment. Freaky animal mouths are an **adaptation** that helps them to hunt, eat, and live! Other animals use **venom** to harm the creatures they bite and sting. **Venom** is the poison that some snakes, spiders, lizards, insects, and similar animals make. Read on to learn about the most dangerous and frightening animal bites! This Danger Scale meter will show how harmful each animal's bite can be to people.

ALLIGATOR SNAPPING TURTLE

Snapping turtles don't have teeth. But they still have a powerful bite! They have a strong beak that helps them chomp on their **prey.** An alligator snapping turtle can bite a broomstick in half—and bite off a person's fingers! It hunts its food with a flashy lure. Attached to its tongue is a small, pink growth that looks like a worm. This tricks fish into swimming right into a snapping turtle's mouth!

DANGER SCALE
LOW

COMMON FANGTOOTH

The common fangtooth is a fish that lives deep in the ocean. It has a large mouth and scary teeth. Its **fangs** (long, sharp teeth) are so big that the fish can never close its mouth completely! The fangtooth's huge mouth helps it to hunt its **prey.**

The fangtooth only grows to about 6 inches (15 cm) long!

AMERICAN ALLIGATOR

The American alligator has strong jaws with many sharp teeth. It uses its strong bite to catch small animals that live in or near the water. The alligator has tiny pits on the sides of its jaws that sense the movements of its **prey!** Once it bites down, it spins and shreds its **prey** to pieces.

VAMPIRE BAT

The vampire bat drinks blood!
It feeds on animals like cows,
chickens, and horses. Sometimes,
the vampire bat will even drink the
blood of humans. The vampire bat
has sharp, triangle-shaped front teeth.
They look like vampire **fangs!**

Bats sense what's around them
through *echolocation*. They make
high-pitched sounds and listen to
how the echoes come back to them.

Whoa!

ASSASSIN BUG

The assassin *(uh SAS uhn)* bug's mouth is shaped like a pointy beak. It pokes its **prey** with its beak and pushes poisonous spit into the **prey.** The spit turns the **prey's** insides to goo! The assassin bug sucks out and eats the insides of its **prey.** Assassin bugs sometimes bite humans, too—and the bites are painful! They can also give dangerous diseases to people. (An assassin is a killer or murderer. This bug's name fits!)

LAMPREY

Lampreys use their sharp teeth to grip their **prey**, like this fish.

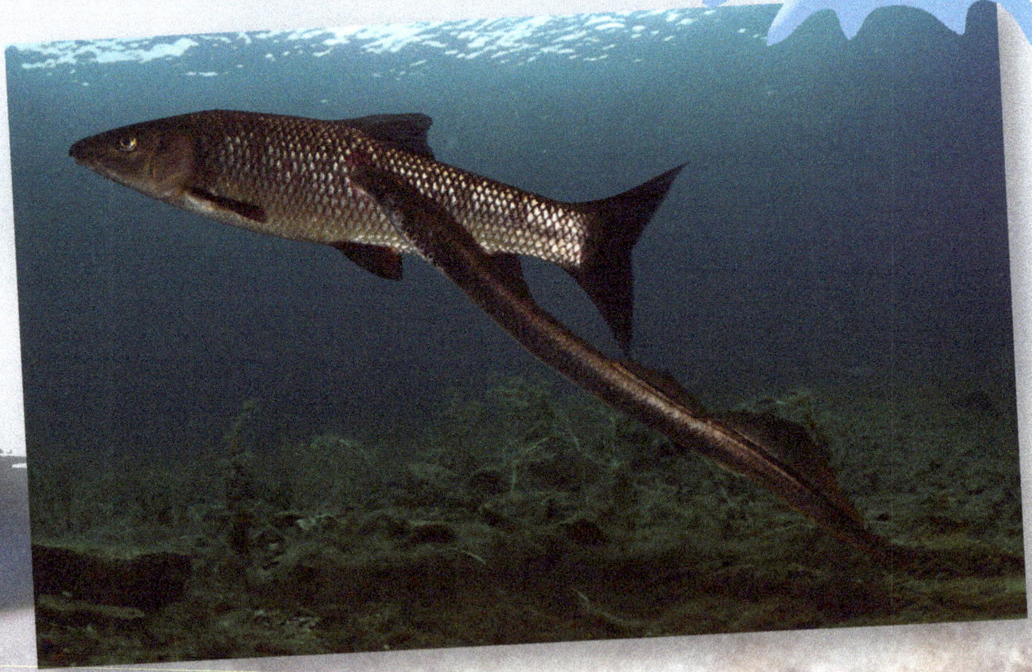

Lampreys are fish with long, thin bodies. They look like snakes. Some lampreys use their scary mouths to suck fluids from the bodies of other fish. These lampreys have lots of horny teeth to bite into their **prey.** Their teeth are arranged in circular rows. They even have teeth on their tongues to rip open skin!

SEA KRAIT

Whoa!

Sea krait can stay underwater
for up to 2 hours to hunt before
coming to the surface to breathe.
The longest a person has held his
breath underwater is around 20 minutes!

The sea krait is a type of snake that lives in and near the ocean. It swims underwater to hunt! Sea kraits have dangerous **venom** that kills their **prey.** They use their long, sharp **fangs** to push the **venom** into their **prey.**

GOOSE

Geese have things in their mouths that look like teeth. They are called tomia. These sharp teeth are on their beaks—and on their tongues! They help geese swallow their food. Geese eat water plants, grass, corn, and wheat.

FANGTOOTH MORAY EEL

Eels are slimy, long, thin fish that look like snakes. The fangtooth moray eel has a long mouth filled with many teeth. Its sharp teeth look like broken glass! The fangtooth moray eel eats shrimp, small fish, and other small sea creatures.

Yuck!

Moray eels have a second set of jaws to help them eat! This other set of jaws pulls the eel's food into its throat.

Terrifying Teeth

Animals' teeth come in lots of shapes and sizes. Animals like elephants have **tusks** (long, pointed teeth). Sharks have rows and rows of teeth. Take a look at some of the most extreme teeth!

Elephant

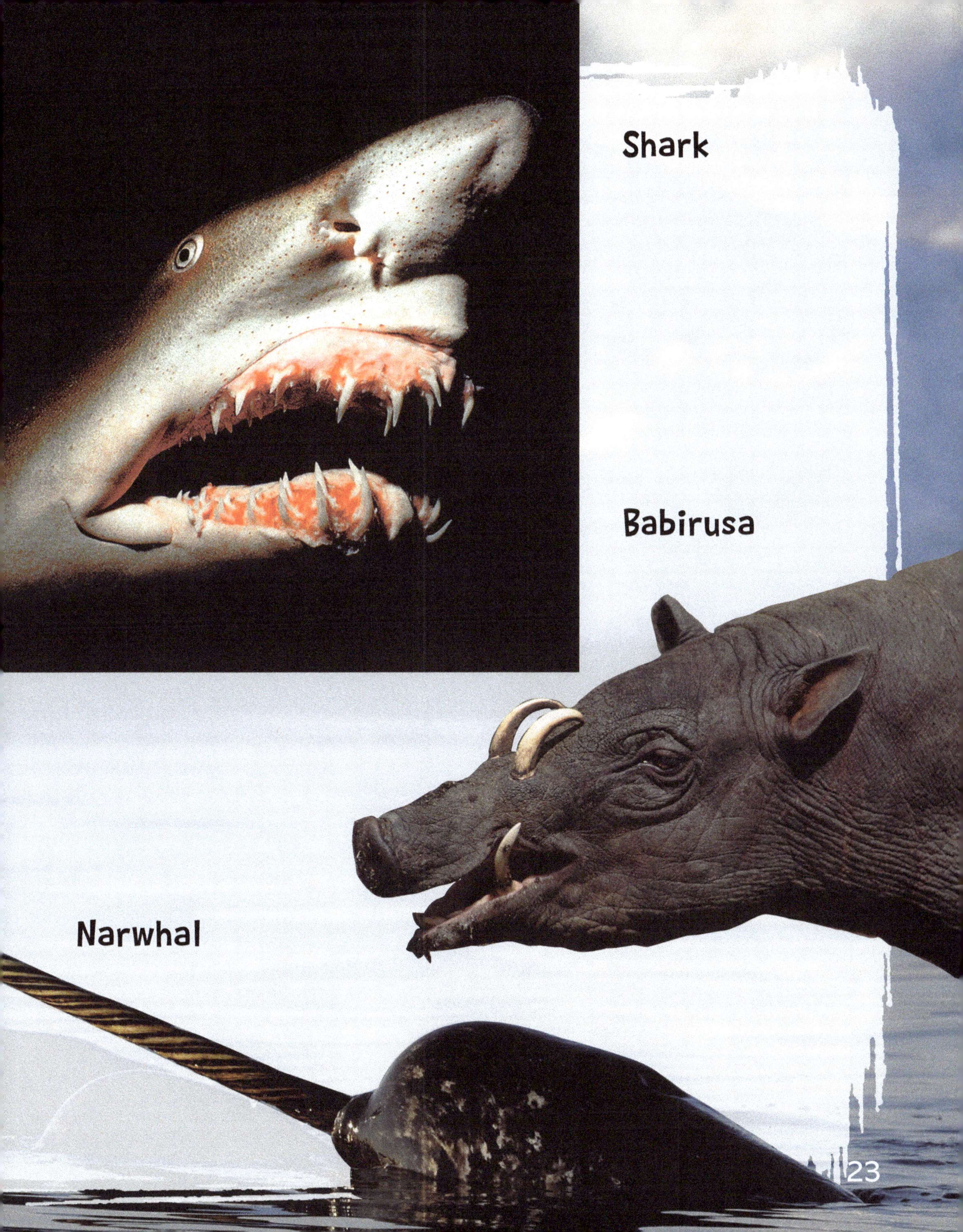

Shark
Babirusa
Narwhal

KOMODO DRAGON

The Komodo dragon is the largest living lizard. It has sharp, pointy teeth. Often, it eats animals that have already died. It uses its tongue to smell the rotting bodies of dead animals from far away. But the Komodo dragon is fast enough to kill large animals, like deer, wild pigs, and even water buffalo!

DANGER SCALE
MEDIUM

ANGLER FISH

Anglerfish have wide mouths and sharp teeth for catching **prey.** An anglerfish lures its **prey** using a spine that hangs from its snout. The snout is the part on the front of an animal's head where the mouth, nose, and jaws are. Anglerfish move the spine back and forth to attract other fish and shrimp to eat. Anglerfish that live in the deep sea where there is little light have spines that glow! Anglerfish can grow to be up to 6 feet (2 meters) long.

VIPER

Vipers are **venomous** (poisonous) snakes. They have a pair of long, hollow **fangs** in their top jaw. They use these scary teeth to push **venom** into their **prey!** They work like needles giving someone a shot. Vipers mostly eat small mammals, birds, and lizards. Vipers also bite to defend themselves.

Vipers can track their **prey** by sensing heat. This is how they would see a mouse!

Dangerous Bites

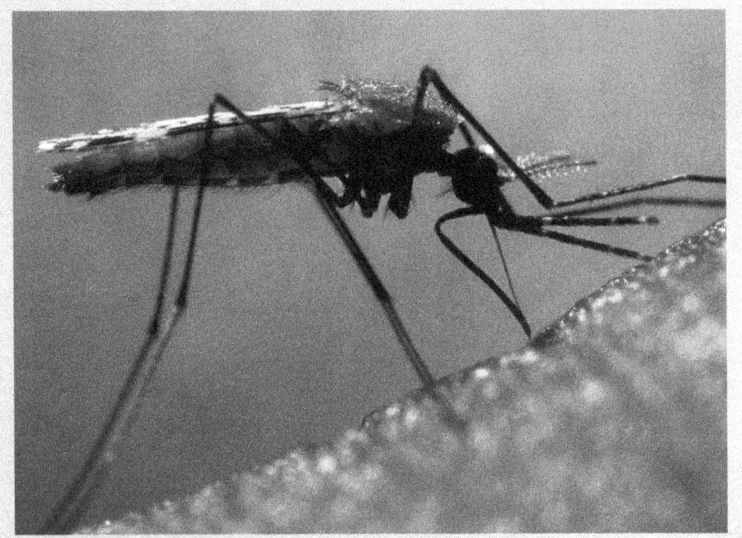

Mosquito

These little insects are among the deadliest animals. They can carry harmful diseases. Mosquitos are responsible for the deaths of millions of people every year.

Hippopotamus

Hippos are huge animals. And they have some of the strongest jaws! Their sharp, jagged teeth and their powerful bite are deadly.

Blue-ringed octopus

These octopusus are **venomous.**
One blue-ringed octopus has
enough poison to kill 26 people!
The **venom** works fast.

King cobra

The king cobra is the longest
venomous snake. The snake's
venom is strong enough to
kill an elephant with one bite!

SAWFISH

The sawfish has a flat body with a long snout called a rostrum *(RAH struhm)*. The rostrum is edged with hard, pointy scales that make it look like a saw. The sawfish uses it to dig in the mud for fish or other things to eat. It also swipes its rostrum back and forth through groups of fish to stab them!

DRAGONFISH

Dragonfish live deep in the ocean. They have large mouths and sharp teeth. A dragonfish's teeth are curved toward the back of its mouth. This is to make it hard for its **prey** to escape!

Dragonfish live so deep in the ocean that no light reaches them. They create their own light! Dragonfish have body parts that work like flashlights to shine light in the dark ocean water.

Menacing Mouths

Mandrill

This type of monkey has a scary-looking mouth. Mandrills have a pair of extra-long teeth on their top and bottom jaws! Mandrills often let out a frightening scream when they open their mouths wide.

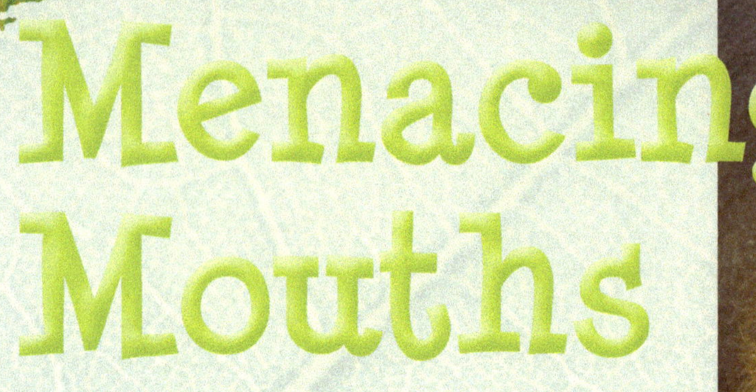

Stag beetle

Stag beetles have huge mouthparts that grow out from their heads and look like antlers.

Snake

Snakes have special jaws that let them swallow food that is larger than their head!

Hagfish

This slimy, skinny fish has a wild mouth! It's filled with rows of pointy teeth.

Grouper

Groupers have huge mouths. They use their mouths like vacuums to suck in food from far away!

MUSK DEER

The musk deer is a type of small deer that lives in the mountains and forests of parts of Asia. It has small **tusks** (long, pointy front teeth) that look like vampire **fangs!**

Musk is a smelly liquid that male musk deer use to mark their territory. For hundreds of years, people have used this liquid in perfumes. Musk deer have been hunted for their musk, and they are almost extinct (all dead).

DANGER SCALE
LOW

VAMPIRE FINCH

The vampire finch is a small bird. It feeds on the blood of other birds when food is scarce. The vampire finch uses its beak to peck at other birds until they bleed!

DANGER SCALE
LOW

BROWN RECLUSE

The brown recluse is one of the most **venomous** spiders in the world. This spider is small, but its bite can do big damage! The brown recluse has a marking in the shape of a violin on its back.

These spiders are about the size of a penny, a small U.S. coin only 3/4 inch (19 mm) across!

POLAR BEAR

Polar bears are huge, white bears of the North. Most big bears have powerful bites. But the polar bear has the strongest and most dangerous of them all! They are skilled hunters who can sniff out their **prey** from miles and miles away.

Glossary

Adaptation

a change in structure, form, or habits to fit different conditions.

Fang

a long, pointed tooth.

Prey

an animal that is hunted, killed, and eaten by another; to hunt, kill, and eat another animal.

Venom

a liquid that an animal makes to stun, injure, or kill another animal through biting or stinging.

Venomous

poisonous; producer of venom.

Tusk

a long, curving tooth that sticks out of the side of the mouth and usually grows in pairs, as in the elephant and walrus.

Index

Acknowledgments

Cover: © Stephen Dalton, Nature Picture Library; © Alex Mustard, Nature Picture Library

4-5 © Daniel Heuclin, Nature Picture Library

6-7 © Solvin Zankl, Nature Picture Library

8-9 © Ingo Arndt, Nature Picture Library

10-11 © Stephen Dalton, Nature Picture Library

12-13 © Jabruson/Nature Picture Library; © Gil Wizen, MYN/Nature Picture Library

14-15 © Nature Production/Nature Picture Library; © Paulo Oliveira, Alamy Images

16-17 © Brandon Cole, Nature Picture Library

18-19 © Bernard Castelein, Nature Picture Library; © Ian Dyball, Shutterstock

20-21 © Alex Mustard, Nature Picture Library

22-23 © Eric Baccega, Nature Picture Library; © Nick Garbutt, Nature Picture Library; © Jeff Rotman, Nature Picture Library; © Anup Shah, Nature Picture Library

24-25 © Will Burrard-Lucas, Nature Picture Library

26-27 © David Shale, Nature Picture Library

28-29 © Barry Mansell, Nature Picture Library; Julius Lab/University of California, San Francisco

30-31 © Martha Holmes, Nature Picture Library; © Warwick Sloss, Nature Picture Library; © Jurgen Freund, Nature Picture Library; © Daniel Heuclin, Nature Picture Library

32-33 © Doug Perrine, Nature Picture Library

34-35 © Solvin Zankl, Nature Picture Library

36-37 © Solvin Zankl, Nature Picture Library; © Mark Bowler, Nature Picture Library; © Terry Whittaker, 2020VISION/Nature Picture Library; © Inaki Relanzon, Nature Picture Library; © Alex Mustard, Nature Picture Library; © Museum of New Zealand Te Papa Tongarewa

38-39 © Mark Bowler, Nature Picture Library; © Vivek Menon, Nature Picture Library

40-41 © Pete Oxford, Nature Picture Library

42-43 © Breck P. Kent, Shutterstock; © Steve Collender, Shutterstock; © Spiroview Inc/Shutterstock

44-45 © Andy Rouse, Nature Picture Library